RAILWAYS OF THE
EAST MIDLANDS

JOHN EVANS

AMBERLEY

By the Same Author

Last Rites: From the Track to the Scrapyard
Workhorses of the Big Four
Railways of Wales in the 1960s
Britain's Railways in Transition 1965–75
Britain's Railways in Transition 1976–90
The Cromford and High Peak Railway in Colour
Great Central Railway: Decline and Fall
Northampton Buses

First published 2022

Amberley Publishing
The Hill, Stroud
Gloucestershire, GL5 4EP

www.amberley-books.com

Copyright © John Evans, 2022

The right of John Evans to be identified as
the Author of this work has been asserted in
accordance with the Copyrights, Designs and
Patents Act 1988.

ISBN 978 1 4456 9890 8 (print)
ISBN 978 1 4456 9891 5 (ebook)

British Library Cataloguing in Publication Data.
A catalogue record for this book is available from
the British Library.

Typesetting by SJmagic DESIGN SERVICES, India.
Printed in Great Britain.

Contents

Introduction

Many photographs have been taken of East Midlands railways over the years. In some ways the region had everything for the railway enthusiast: five main lines, endless fascinating cross-country routes and rural branches, plus a plethora of industrial quarries and coal mines. Despite this it fares less well in terms of railway publishing, possibly because it has none of the spectacular banks or mountain scenery you will find in the west and north of England, Wales or Scotland. The railway network in the East Midlands was intense – you were never far from a station, and some modest-sized communities benefitted from two or three. Dominating it all was the Midland Railway, whose small-engine policy left its mark right up to the end of steam, with plenty of veteran 0-6-0s at work well into the 1960s. When diesels took over, it seemed as though Sulzer products dominated. The Peak class operated the majority of fast passenger services and many freights for twenty years, and their Type 2 sisters were

The classic Midland signal box, seen here at Ravenstone Wood Junction, near Olney.

everywhere. There were also the delightful idiosyncrasies. The first ten Peaks – named after mountains – trundled around Nottinghamshire and elsewhere for many years on coal trains. Derby works and its busy station were a centre for eager enthusiasts for decades, and even today might produce the odd surprise. Elderly diesel units seemed an ideal companion for those huge twin-post telegraph poles that lined many Midland lines. And a Midland signal box was as handsome as anything designed by the other major railways.

But the Midland Railway never had it entirely its own way. The Great Northern, London & North Western and Great Central railways, plus several minor concerns, were looked upon as intruders at Derby, but also played their part in serving the six counties of the region. This book takes you on a nostalgic stroll through what were certainly twenty years of major change on the railways of the region.

The East Midlands

Most of us seem to live in a clearly defined part of the country. If you reside east of either the A1 or the East Coast main line between London and Peterborough, you are in East Anglia. Should you call home somewhere in that space between Liverpool, Manchester and the Scottish border you are basically in the North West. But what if you live in Northampton, where I spent about half of my life? Turn on your TV and the news will be a cheery voice from Norwich telling you that someone has lost a handbag in Great Yarmouth. My daughter lives only 12 miles away in Silverstone and her 'local' TV news comes from Oxford, with reports that the Isle of Wight ferry is running late. You could drive from Glossop to the Wash and be in the East Midlands all the way; or from Chesterfield to Brackley. Author Anthony J. Lambert includes Buckinghamshire, Warwickshire and Staffordshire in his definition of the region. No wonder we East Midlanders feel a little confused and stateless.

The East Midlands by official regional definition comprises the counties of Derbyshire, Leicestershire, much of Lincolnshire, Northamptonshire, Nottinghamshire and Rutland. Its largest cities and towns are Leicester, Nottingham and Derby, plus Lincoln, Mansfield and Northampton, but there are a dozen or more other important ones, from Skegness to Hinckley and from Chesterfield to Wellingborough.

Certain benefits accrue from this somewhat vague boundary. The East Midlands has dozens of railway lines, even today. It has the West Coast, East Coast, Midland and Great Western (just) main lines passing through it, and once had the Great Central as well. Built on coal and iron ore, it has also been a great generator of freight, with huge swathes of agriculture, hungry power stations, extensive manufacturing and widespread mining all forming part of the mix. At the time of writing it is the fastest growing region of Britain outside London.

All this, of course, means that it has an interesting railway history. This book will focus on the period from the mid-1960s to the mid-1980s – a period that witnessed a severe decline in freight and a 'rebalancing' of passenger traffic. But much of what was fascinating still remained. Once Dr Beeching had axed the cross-country routes and some main lines as well, plus many branches, the region still had a fairly intensive rail network.

As a schoolboy, we used to stump up *7s 6d* (37.5p) of our hard-earned cash each year for a holiday runabout ticket. My funds came from a delivery round on a wobbly bicycle for noted butcher Mr Cheney, during which the only moment of amusement was a young mum in a daring nightie who lived in Vernon Terrace. We vied for the honour of this delivery… but I am losing track.

My runabout ticket covered a wide area of the East Midlands – from Northampton to Wellingborough, north to Matlock, west to Tamworth and all the lines in-between. In those days that was as much railway as you could reasonably expect to cover in a week, especially if you came home every night as we did (we were still at school). A typical day might mean going from Northampton Castle to Rugby Midland, walking to Rugby Central and travelling to Nottingham Victoria; from there we might travel to Nottingham Midland on a trolley bus, then visit Derby, go to Matlock and back, head for Leicester London Road and then end up at Wellingborough Midland Road. Finally, we could catch the last push-pull train of the day home to Northampton Castle. We sometimes paid for an extra ticket to places like Sheffield or Doncaster.

Much of that network has gone, especially the east to west routes. But I travelled over many of the old lines a few months ago, visiting Nottingham, Derby, Lincoln, Worksop, Newark, Matlock and Leicester. Everything has changed, and we sometimes lament those differences, but they are not always for the worse. The Midland main line, the heart of the region, is very busy with a huge choice of trains; a regional three-day rover ticket is still as cheap as chips. And the character of many of the towns and cities remains the same, as does the Peak District. It's time, however, to take a look back and find out more about the old days.

The beating heart of the East Midlands was the old Midland Railway, whose main line ran like a spine from Irchester in south Northamptonshire to the northern borders of Nottinghamshire and Derbyshire. Open up an atlas of pre-grouping lines and it is amazing just how much space the rails of the Midland Railway occupy. In the far south it reaches Bristol, and its crimson engines could be found steaming into Carlisle, Wolverhampton, Peterborough and Lincoln. It was also an enthusiastic participant in joint lines – the long rambling partnership with the Great Northern that reached Yarmouth and, most famous of all, the wonderful Somerset and Dorset. The Midland Railway certainly interpreted its title with spectacular latitude. Hamilton Ellis, that shrewd observer of the railways a hundred years ago, was definitive about the Midland Railway. It had, he stated, the best stations in England and the most comfortable third-class carriages. 'It believed in lightly-loaded expresses. There were frequent, fast services and some of them contrived to be very fast, in spite of a peculiar undersizedness of its locomotives.' Hamilton Ellis makes a good point. Stand by the lineside at Kegworth, for example, in the last years of the Midland and you would soon realise the motive power department used nothing larger than four-coupled engines for passenger trains and 0-6-0s for freight. If more power was needed, the Midland resorted as a matter of course to double-heading. 'The Midland managed without breakdown or disrepute,' says Ellis. 'Indeed, it was a railway which stood very highly in the public favour.' The excellence of its rolling stock resulted from a focus on making passengers comfortable. This philosophy also helped to create fine stations where it was no trouble to linger. Of course, St Pancras was its greatest, but even minor stations had a degree of elegance and careful thought not always present in rural edifices. Stamford's Tudor-style building with its splendid tower is a handsome example. Cromford was Italianate and a wonderful place to wait for a train. Or deliberately miss one.

The vast frontage of Leicester London Road is simply splendid, as was its platform-mounted signal box and giant clock, although its 'island platforms in a cutting' layout lacked the panache of some of its competitors. Further north, Loughborough Midland was also a delight in the 1960s, but has since been unfortunately rather 'rationalised'. Kettering's wonderful awnings and ironwork are equally remarkable. Melton Mowbray Town, Buxton, Collingham, Northampton St John's Street and Mansfield Town were all were worth visiting, and we will meet some of them in the photographs that follow this narrative.

Mention must also be made of Midland Railway footbridges. There was nothing quite like a sweeping Midland footbridge, with its intricate lattice ironwork. Such elegance made a Midland footbridge so much more than just a way of switching platforms, and happily many survive. Also distinctive were the signal boxes, with their elegant proportions and four-piece, 'hipped' roofs. And all its main routes were lined by those attractive telegraph poles with twin supports.

Yet the Midland never had the East Midlands entirely to itself. It was to some extent squeezed by the London & North Western Railway to the west and the Great Northern Railway to the east. In fact, the Midland main line, for all its prowess and efficiency, veered rather suspiciously to the west and the east. Here, after the creation of the Big Four, it would watch enviously as famous high-speed trains, hauled by the finest express engines in the country, competed to carry passengers between London and the most important cities in the North West, North East and Scotland. The Midland Railway had arrived late on the scene, not reaching London with its own metals until 1868, having previously used both the east coast (Great Northern via Bedford and Hitchin) and west coast (London & North Western from Leicester to Rugby) main lines to reach England's capital. Once its main line was complete – with the opening of the Settle to Carlisle railway in 1876 – the Midland at last had a chance to say it had a trunk route from London to Scotland. Not only that, but its sumptuous trains departed from St Pancras, instantly one of the finest stations in Britain, to both Glasgow and Edinburgh.

Once the old companies were grouped into the Big Four, the Midland's way of doing things, which had initially been imposed on the new monolithic LMS railway, began to show its limitations. True, it had a strong influence on the newly formed giant in its early days, with Derby usurping Crewe in terms of locomotive design and everything painted that handsome Midland red, but the LMS was a fast-changing animal and by the mid-1930s, as one of the world's largest companies, it was taking a more independent stance. Midland domination waned and Stanier's fleet of new hi-tech engines made some of the Derby products look obsolete overnight. Fowler's lumbering 7F 0-8-0 of 1929, for example, was totally eclipsed by rival 2-8-0 products from the Great Western and Great Central built decades earlier. Stanier soon showed how it should be done.

For all its comfort and pragmatism, the Midland never truly competed with the east and west route companies, at least not in terms of speed. When the streamlined, high-speed era came, the Midland missed out. Stanier provided an excellent medium-sized express engine, the Jubilee, which was ideal for the more lightly loaded

Midland line expresses. They took over from the Midland Compounds and ran right to the early 1960s, when they in turn handed over to the Peak class diesels, which themselves gave twenty years' service on the main Midland expresses. Eventually these yielded in the 1980s to high-speed trains, although, like the Jubilees before them, the Peaks never enjoyed a complete monopoly of the Midland main line.

Geographically, the Midland Railway strove to dominate Leicestershire, Derbyshire and Nottinghamshire. But there was always someone wanting to slide an annoying tentacle into its territory. Such intruders form some of the most interesting historical network developments, and today we might wonder why so much was spent on new tracks to gain so little. The LNWR and GNR were the main perpetrators. These two companies had the audacity to build a joint line right through the heart of Leicestershire, allowing trains to run from Northampton Castle to Nottingham London Road Low Level. This did not worry the Midland very much as it was a route few people wanted to use; in fact, passenger trains were withdrawn in the early 1950s. But it did carry useful amounts of iron ore and served a big quarry at Scalford. As if an affront to the Midland, the joint line companies built a splendid station at Melton Mowbray (North) and, strangely, another oversized edifice at the small village of Redmile in the Vale of Belvoir serving a couple of farms and some hunting dogs. This joint line also allowed the Great Northern to fulfil one of its aims: to reach Leicester. Here they constructed the impressive station of Belgrave Road, with twin train sheds from which regular excursions to the east coast ran until 1962 when the precarious nature of the track on the branch forced its closure. By then normal passenger services had been withdrawn for ten years, but there is a delicious irony in the fact that the last of these were often hauled by ex-Midland Railway 4-4-0s. Of course, the Midland was not averse to probing other people's territory itself. Its partnership with the Great Northern sent a dreamy long-distance line all the way to Great Yarmouth.

Between Derby, Nottingham and Sheffield, the Midland served a vast number of collieries – there were freight lines everywhere. Once again, the Midland faced some competition. The Great Northern had its own colliery routes, reaching as far north as Langwith Junction, north of Mansfield. At one time the engine shed here had a vast fleet of freight locomotives, many migrating here in the 1960s as other sheds closed their doors. In 1965 there were twenty-two 9F 2-10-0s at Langwith, but these had replaced no fewer than eighty-four Robinson O4 2-8-0s and their O1 Thompson rebuilds, which had been allocated to Langwith over the years. In steam days if you glanced over a railway bridge in north Derbyshire and Nottinghamshire, an O4 or a Fowler 4F with coal wagons would be along within a few minutes.

The other (and rather more annoying) trespasser on what the Midland saw as its personal domain was the Great Central, in many respects a latecomer to the party. Having been the rather less grand Manchester, Sheffield & Lincolnshire Railway (MSL) in the late nineteenth century, it was at that time something of an irritation, but nothing more. It busied itself with a fairly horizontal network of routes, searching for an identity that it got when the eager and ambitious railway promoter Sir Edward Watkin decided that what the MSL really needed was a way of reaching London. And not just London. Watkin had his sights set on burying under the English Channel as well, so his vision was of something that amounted to a Victorian combination of HS2 and the Eurostar. The Midland must have sat up and taken notice when they first saw Nottingham's Victoria station, one of the finest outside London. Not only that, but the Great Central also served cities that the Midland saw as its exclusive preserve, such as Sheffield, Nottingham and Leicester; however, Hamilton Ellis says that initially the London extension of the GCR was viewed as a 'branch line'. It was regarded with pessimism at the time of its inception, he says, especially with regard to its financial prospects. 'If MSL had stood for Money Sunk and Lost, GC clearly meant Gone Completely.' Yet, as Ellis observes, the GC trains were rather lightly loaded but smartly timed, with opulently decorated rolling stock. Its London suburban carriages were 'easily the best in Britain', and yet this was a railway of two halves.

The Manchester expresses were superb and Chief Mechanical Engineer John Robinson provided a very handsome and efficient group of 4-4-0s and 2-8-0s to run freight and passenger services (his elegant Atlantics and 4-6-0s weren't quite such a hit). Yet the trains on the old Manchester, Sheffield and Lincolnshire lines still retained more than a whiff of nineteenth-century rurality about them. Even in its last few years, before Dr Beeching did what the Midland would have liked to have done and shut it, Great Central freights raced through the East Midlands at a speed that the Midland could never have conceived. And it wasn't the engine at the front that made the difference as both railways latterly used the same Class 9F 2-10-0s. It was the operating philosophy and the eagerness of crews that was different.

Derbyshire

Mention Derbyshire railways and many minds would spring to the Midland Railway north of Derby. Few lines can equal it for spectacular scenery and punishing terrain. It was over this route, from Derby to Manchester, that the Midland tried to compete with both the Great Central and London & North Western Railways for the prosperous business traffic between London and Manchester. The four tracks between Derby and Ambergate gave no indication of the work ahead, as the more timid route to Chesterfield swung north-east at the triangular station and the Manchester route cut through the hills towards the Peak District. Initially the going was not too bad as the line ran through the Derwent Valley, but the succession of tunnels, 1 in 100 gradients, cloying cuttings and limestone hills encased the railway and made work for the fireman hard. It was here that the Black 5s and Jubilees shone, putting in impressive daily performances before blasting out over the amazing Monsal Dale Viaduct, and then on upwards to Chapel-en-le-Frith and Manchester Central. To those of us who knew the line, its closure was a catastrophe, overshadowed at the time, perhaps, by the fight for the Waverley route and the closure of the Great Central. Certainly, as Howard Anderson, says, 'one of the most beautiful railway journeys in Britain is no longer possible'.

If you wish to go the Midland way to Manchester today you will have to travel from St Pancras to Sheffield and then cross the Peak by the line through Edale – itself a very rewarding experience, but hardly the same thing as that blast through the Bakewell and Millers Dale. The southern section from Derby to Matlock survives as a withered branch that gives no real impression of a damp autumn day behind a Jubilee or Peak on a Manchester express. Peak Rail are doing their best, but making slow progress with their project to reopen a section of the line, reflecting the challenges of the terrain and such inevitabilities as lost bridges. They already run trains from Matlock to Rowsley, which is quite an achievement. Buxton still offers a rail service north to Manchester and it takes about an hour, but misses out on the grandeur of the old main line.

The Midland was surrounded by a number of London & North Western lines in the area. Among these was the wonderful branch from Ashbourne to Buxton, now the Tissington Trail and the Cromford and High Peak Railway (also a leisure footpath today). Quite how this line, with its cable-worked inclines serving quarries, came to survive for so long is one of the delights of the 1960s (see *The Cromford and High Peak Railway in Colour*). Freights still run into the Peak District, working limestone trains out of the quarry at Hindlow, and an impressive sight they make.

Along the county's borders with Leicestershire and Nottinghamshire, a very different type of railway existed. These carried freight trains on both main and secondary lines, including merry-go-round services to power stations and branch freights.

A brief word about Ilkeston. It was once served by no fewer than four stations, but lost them all and then found itself back on the rail network when a new station was opened in 2017. By then it was one of the largest British towns without a railway station.

Derby itself was always one of the great railway centres. Stand on the platform today and you may see an unusual train or locomotive arriving, befitting its status as the home of railway engineering. There is much railway-related activity in Derby, even today, but the days when all eyes were pressed to the window as a train entered Derby to see what was standing outside the works have sadly gone. Our little group used to mimic the station announcer: 'Derby, Derby, this is Derby,' even before we got off our train. You might expect that no other railway would have the temerity to enter this Midland Railway fortress. But the Great Northern was no respecter of rank and power, and its roundabout route – covered in the section on Nottinghamshire – ran through Derby Friargate station on its way to Egginton and Staffordshire.

Mineral wagons pass through Derby on 2 August 1965 behind 8F No. 48690 with that well-known bridge above the train.

A Banbury 9F, which excited local spotters, breaks the monotony of 8Fs and WDs at Derby on 2 August 1965.

Buxton shed is still full of steam on 30 June 1966. A visitor from Birkenhead is this ex-Crosti 9F, No. 92023, which had arrived on an express freight.

Also at Buxton shed on 30 June 1966 is 2-8-0 No. 48744, which lasted to the end of steam at the depot and saw more service after that.

Once this LNWR edifice was one of a matching (but not identical) pair of stations at Buxton with elegant fan windows, but only the low wall remains of the Midland Railway station. From the LNWR station you usually travelled north; the Midland station served stations to the south.

The last day special on the Cromford and High Peak Railway with two J94 tanks, Nos 68012 and 68006, is about to stall on the notorious 1 in 14 Hopton incline on 30 April 1967. The train was divided in two and managed to complete the climb. (Bryan Jeyes)

Working a Sunday engineering train along the Hope Valley line at Edale is shunter No. 3988 on 8 April 1972.

At Matlock Bath a diesel unit for Matlock is about to start the last stage of its journey on 28 July 1972. It is hard to imagine that not long before this, we would be looking at a main line.

On 28 July 1972 a ballast train enters Derby station behind Class 37 diesel No. 37164.

The north end of Derby station with Class 45/0 No. 45013 arriving with a southbound express on 22 February 1982.

This train is near Whaley Bridge, north of Buxton, on 17 June 1983. The train is on the old LNWR route to Manchester, which plunged into Midland territory.

On a murky December day in 1966, a freight double-headed by 2-8-0 No. 48681 and 2-10-0 No. 92022 blasts through the mist at Cromford. (Bryan Jeyes)

Derby Friargate in 1967 three years after closure. It was on the Derbyshire and Staffordshire Extension of the Great Northern Railway, which upset the Midland Railway as it went right into their headquarters of Derby. (Bryan Jeyes)

The less than salubrious platform buildings at Pear Tree and Normanton on the Derby to Birmingham main line seen in March 1968 just before closure. It reopened in 1976. (Bryan Jeyes)

A Peak diesel passes Repton and Willington station, Derbyshire, on 24 February 1968. Closed a few days later, it reopened in 1984 with new buildings. (Bryan Jeyes)

Millers Dale station, Derbyshire, with a diesel multiple unit waiting to depart for Buxton Midland on 25 February 1967. The station closed a couple of weeks later and is recalled in the Flanders and Swann song 'Slow Train.' (Bryan Jeyes)

Our diesel unit has now reached Buxton Midland from Millers Dale. The station disappeared under a road scheme. (Bryan Jeyes)

Buxton LNWR station with its overall roof, which was later removed. The Midland station is on the left. (Bryan Jeyes)

0-4-0 saddle tank No. 47000 shunts at Sheep Pasture on the Cromford and High Peak line. The wagons will descend to Cromford on a rope-worked (actually steel cable) incline. (Bryan Jeyes)

Wagons ascend the Sheep Pasture incline from Cromford on 21 December 1966. (Bryan Jeyes)

A pair of the very useful Class 20 locomotives Nos 20049 and 20060 pass through Chinley on 19 June 1986 with cement wagons. (David Hird)

A wonderfully atmospheric shot at Cadley Hill Colliery, Derbyshire, on 2 November 1979 with Bagnall 0-6-0ST *Empress*, the star of the show. (Bob Mullins)

A brand new experimental multiple unit, No. 151002, stands at Ambergate, a once superb station.

Leicestershire

The railways of Leicestershire centre closely on the county's principal city. The dominant line is the Midland, which runs from Market Harborough in the south to Loughborough in the north. The Midland also has an important junction north of the city at Syston, from which a link to Melton Mowbray was offered. East of this pleasant market town was another junction, allowing trains to make the direct journey across south Lincolnshire and Norfolk to Great Yarmouth using the Midland and Great Northern Joint Line through South Lynn and Melton Constable. Today the journey from Leicester to the East Coast, changing at Peterborough and Norwich, will take you around five hours. But assuming you do not wish to head into the far reaches of East Anglia, a route aiming south-east passes through Oakham and Stamford, ending up at Peterborough. This line is open today and forms an important east–west link across the Midlands, joining Birmingham to Cambridge and Norwich. Crucially, it is the first real east–west link north of London and will remain so until the Oxford to Cambridge line (now called the East West Rail project) is reinstated.

The Midland also owned a fascinating line that ran west from Leicester to coal mines at Swannington, a real pioneering route that was opened in 1832. It had its own terminus in Leicester at West Bridge and ran through the very tight Glenfield Tunnel, over a mile long and with what must have been the tightest clearances of any tunnel on the main rail network. Coal trains from West Bridge to Coalville squeezed into the tunnel headed by a few veteran Midland 0-6-0s retained specially for the purpose. Eventually, British Railways modified the cabs of a couple of Standard Class 2 2-6-0s to fit. It was a line that time (and British Railways) forgot, surviving until 1966. All trains then ran through to Knighton Junction to join the Midland main line. You can still enjoy a tour of the tunnel today, hosted by the enterprising members of Leicester Industrial Historical Society. The later section eventually ran through to Burton-on-Trent, closing to passengers in 1964. It is still open for freight, however, and there is talk of passengers returning. The remaining Midland route in Leicestershire is the closed Leicester to Rugby line. This formed part of the Midland's first attempt to reach London and stories are told of Midland trains being deliberately held up before managing to encroach upon North Western metals at Rugby. After a few years of glory, the railway settled down to become an undistinguished branch with some poor stations and an imposing entry into Rugby over a substantial viaduct. Passenger trains were latterly mainly hauled by

Fowler 2-6-4 tank engines. Once these disappeared in 1962 the line survived for three years as a freight route, although lightly used. The big viaduct at Rugby still survives and there has been talk in recent years of reopening the line, although it is hardly high priority.

The other main player was the Great Central, whose main line was opened through the city in 1899. The creation of this route meant skimming across the top of the city, and the civil engineering work required to achieve this was remarkable. After the line closed in 1969, much of this vast quantity of superbly laid brickwork was removed and the city seemed to undergo a visual change as enormous as when the Great Central was built. The contrast between the Midland and Great Central routes could hardly have been greater. Midland trains burrowed through cuttings and bridges before arriving at London Road, a rather unimpressive structure from platform level with two large island platforms. The best thing about it was the west signal box, mounted on one of the platforms, and its wonderful clock mounted above. From road level it is a much happier proposition, with delicious arches, multicoloured brickwork and a splendid domed tower at the north end. Contrast this with Leicester Central, where trains swept at high speed across the rooftops of the city and braked to a halt. A regular point for an engine change, this would be accomplished amazingly quickly, with trains efficiently off and on their way. A summer Saturday was a Mecca for spotters, with endless trains heading from the East Midlands and the north to the south coast. In the 1950s and '60s you could see a wonderful variety of engines, from Western types coming up from Banbury to Gresley Pacifics, BR Standards of many types and a continuous flow of freights. Central station was also ornate, with a row of gables and a substantial tower (to show the Midland it meant business?). Sadly, much of it, including all the platform area, has gone, but recently Leicester has decided it still has an element of affection for its old station and the remaining frontage (regrettably devoid of tower and gables) has been preserved as part of an 'entertainment village' with a bowling alley and food hall.

The other intruder in the Midland's Leicestershire territory was the Great Northern and London & North Western Joint Line. It was a fascinating enterprise, and I make no apology for including a number of pictures of it. What could be more pleasant than spending rather too much of a day rambling through high Leicestershire on a leisurely journey from Northampton to Nottingham?

Leicester shed yard on 2 August 1965. Under the coaling plant is 2-6-0 No. 76043, which ended up at Machynlleth, with Sulzer Type 2 diesels alongside.

Class 45 No. 121 leaves for the north at Market Harborough on 29 September 1972. The lines on the left led to Rugby and Northampton, but the missing signal arm tells the story – they were only used for occasional freight trains at this time.

Melton Mowbray had two very nice stations. Approaching the Midland one is a Swindon three-car multiple unit on 7 July 1972.

This is the other, rather grander, Melton station: Melton Mowbray North on the old GN and LNWR Joint Line. On 12 November 1966, after closure, we can see the splendid coat of arms on the end gable and the huge canopy.

Wigston South with the railway infrastructure in excellent condition. 'Peak' diesel No. 45122 passes on 17 September 1978 heading for St Pancras.

This is Loughborough Midland station on 18 September 1979 and Class 45/1 No. 45133 is heading north with a long passenger train. The closed Great Central line passes over the bridge, which was later demolished and is now being rebuilt.

Approaching Hinckley on 7 July 1983 is Class 31 No. 31272 on a holiday train running from the East Coast to the Midlands. A succession of these used the Leicester–Birmingham line each summer.

On the recently closed Great Central main line, this is a lovely view of Abbey Lane signal box in June 1969. (Bryan Jeyes)

A diesel multiple unit trundles along the Great Central near Swithland on the section now reopened by preservationists. (Bryan Jeyes)

The busy 11.02 to Nottingham arrives at Leicester Central on 29 April 1967. (Adam Jones)

Still standing in June 1969 is Leicester Central engine shed (38C). Closed in 1964, it once housed the top express engines, including *Flying Scotsman*. (Bryan Jeyes)

A diesel unit leaves Lutterworth on the Great Central in April 1969, and the single passenger who alighted crosses the tracks. The freight yard has been removed and all is lost. (Bryan Jeyes)

Belgrave and Birstall was another Great Central station and is seen here in 1969. This was the first GC station north of Leicester. (Bryan Jeyes)

Leicester Belgrave Road, the Great Northern Railway station, derelict on 12 November 1966. Before closure in 1962 it came alive every summer with crowds heading for the east coast resorts.

The first station on the Great Northern branch to Leicester Belgrave Road was Humberstone, seen here four years after closure on a damp 12 November 1966.

Ingarsby was opened in 1882 and closed to regular passenger traffic in 1953. The building survives today as a private home. It was also on the Great Northern branch to Leicester Belgrave Road. (Bryan Jeyes)

A station not many will remember – this is John O'Gaunt on the old GN and LNWR Joint Line just south of Melton Mowbray. A graceful fourteen-arch viaduct lies beyond the platforms.

Blaby station was on the Birmingham to Peterborough line and closed in 1968, two days after this picture was taken. (Bryan Jeyes)

Elmsthorpe on the Birmingham to Peterborough route. Another station that closed in 1968 but has not reopened. (Bryan Jeyes)

Leicester London Road at night with 'Peak' No. D70 making an appearance. Notice the impressive clock. (Bryan Jeyes)

No. 56037 among merry-go-round wagons at Coalville's open day on 20 August 1978. (Bob Mullins)

Lilbourne's neat and tidy station on the Rugby to Peterborough line on 4 June 1966. Sadly, this was the last day of business. (Bryan Jeyes)

Syston, a busy and important junction, lost its station in 1968, but it was reopened in 1994 as a rather feeble single platform. Shortly before it closed, a Sulzer Type 2 diesel passes with a parcels train. (Bryan Jeyes)

After so many sad pictures, here we see the lovely old Director 4-4-0 *Butler-Henderson* back on Great Central metals on the revived heritage railway in the early 1980s.

Class 45 No. 45150 at Leicester awaiting its next duty in autumn 1985. (Bob Mullins)

An HST pauses at Leicester and mailbags are sorted – once part of everyday station life. (Bob Mullins)

A night-time shot of a newly delivered Sprinter waiting to leave Leicester station in the mid-1980s. (Bob Mullins)

Flying Scotsman leaves Leicester London Road on 22 February 1969 when it was Britain's only main-line steam locomotive. It was running with two tenders to extend its range. (Bryan Jeyes)

Lincolnshire

The Lincolnshire Wolds Railway is one of the more modest heritage lines. Like many others, it has big ambitions. While the short ride from Ludborough to North Thoresby and back is a very pleasant experience, it gives no sense of the importance of this once busy through route, which carried expresses from Cleethorpes to Kings Cross, many local services and a great deal of freight. After being listed for closure in the Beeching cuts, there was a lengthy fight that resulted in defeat for the railway protagonists. Much of the line was closed to passengers in 1970 and just the Boston to Firsby section remained open to allow trains from the East Midlands to reach Skegness. The closure left Louth as the biggest town in Lincolnshire without a railway station, housing a population of 17,000 people.

Lincolnshire, being a more sparse, agricultural county, had a smaller railway network than others in the East Midlands. The southern end of the county was dominated by the Great Northern Railway; the Great Central held sway in the north and in the important port area around Grimsby. Closures wreaked havoc in the 1960s; east of Sleaford and Lincoln almost the only surviving route is that to Skegness, which prospered because of the railway and in particular holiday traffic from industrial East Midlands towns and cities. Even so, Beeching had it – and many other east Lincolnshire lines – on his 'hit list'. Lines serving resorts in the Mablethorpe area failed to survive closures in the area in 1970. Happily, the Spalding–Sleaford–Lincoln line survives and is a happy trip in my experience, with a great 'community' feel as a single-car unit potters across the county heading for Peterborough. Lincoln itself was served by a multitude of railways: the Great Central, Great Northern and Great Eastern all laid claims on the city's population; the Midland, being the Midland, was there too, with its own station, St Marks.

In what used to be South Humberside, the railways have fared better. Grimsby, Immingham and Scunthorpe are still important railheads, but no longer enjoy the same connections to the south of the old days. But the railways are busy, the Drax Power Station attracting biomass brought in by rail and Scunthorpe still an important steel-making centre.

Dividing Lincolnshire from the rest of the East Midlands, symbolically if not exactly on a county line, is the East Coast main line. Retford, Newark, Grantham and Little Bytham recall the pre-war days of steam streamliners, and today, as an electrified high-speed line with the latest motive power, its tradition is being continued. In the period we are considering in this volume the Deltics were the prime motive power, supported by the Class 47s, but pictures in the early 1970s still show a railway lined by telegraph poles and controlled by old semaphore signalling. It was here, of course, that the A4 4-6-2 *Mallard* rocketed down Stoke Bank in 1937 and set a never-to-be beaten speed record for a steam locomotive.

Lastly, a mention of a Lincolnshire survivor. This is the line from Cleethorpes to New Holland and Barton-on-Humber. Definitely worth the effort, even if the terminus station is a sad disappointment; the ride getting there most certainly is not.

On 7 July 1972 an Up train halts at Grantham right next to the signal box. The engine is Class 47 No. 1108, still in green livery.

In 1979 a special heads over Welland Bridge, Spalding, behind Class 33 No. 33053 with a 'Pleasure Seeker' train. (David Hird)

Brush Type 4 No. 1871 heads a Cleethorpes train at Grantham on 7 July 1972. In the bay is a diesel unit with a connecting service for Skegness.

Deltic No. 55007 *Pinza* arrives at Grantham on a morning train to York on 2 November 1979. Just two years' service remained for these powerful machines. (Bob Mullins)

Class 47 No. 47144 leaves Spalding on 12 May 1979 after the flower festival and takes the line to March. These specials were so popular the yard at Spalding would be full of stock. (David Hird)

Class 37 No. 37082 leaves Spalding with a flower parade special on 12 May 1980. This view has changed out of all recognition today. (David Hird)

A view of Class 47 No. 47191 passing Helpringham on the Sleaford to Spalding line on 28 August 1982. The classic combination is a blue locomotive and blue and grey Mk 1 coaches. (David Hird)

The old RAF airfield at Binbrook was a strange resting place for Merchant Navy Pacific No. 35011 *General Steam Navigation*. It is now being restored to its original condition. (Bob Mullins)

On 7 July 1972 at Stamford the Hitchin to Nuneaton empty ballast train heads west hauled by Brush Type 2 No. 5650.

A cross-country service departs west from Stamford in 1986 headed by a Class 47 diesel. (Bob Mullins)

The start of a new generation. Where once there was a great variety of steam locomotives, now we have a new Sprinter, No. 150142, on a local leaving Stamford. (Bob Mullins)

Northamptonshire

As we saw at the beginning of this book, Northamptonshire was a county with a confused identity. The main railway was undoubtedly the London & North Western, with its main line through the county plus branches, one of the which trailed all along the Nene Valley (pronounced 'Nen' in Northampton and a rather posher 'Neen' if you live near Peterborough). While the Midland main line, with its four tracks as far as Kettering, was the star of the show, its Northamptonshire branch lines were a less rewarding group. Most of them failed to survive long enough for Dr Beeching to finish them off. The most interesting was that from Bedford to Northampton, which ran over a series of switchbacks and gave a lively Ivatt 2-6-2T with two coaches the chance to really have some fun charging up and down the hills. The line also had very fine stations, such as that at Olney and its St John's Street terminus right next to Northampton town centre. This closed in 1939 when all services were diverted into the main Castle station, but I recall it still standing in the 1950s, with a forest of elegant chimneys and a dramatic portico. Below the station was a series of small businesses installed in arches that supported the platforms. Later, when just the platforms remained, I met the noted railway photographer Les Hanson there one evening, both of us having squeezed past advert hoardings sited in such a way as to try to keep trespassers out. He told me of the station's latter days, when veteran LNWR express engines were used on the line as a kind of retirement home. The Northampton–Bedford line had some sort of notoriety when both railbuses and diesel multiple units were used to try to cut costs, but could not manage the gradients in winter. So its final months saw a return to steam.

The Midland also had a lengthy line that meandered through the undulating countryside east of Kettering. It eventually reached Huntingdon, having passed through some delightful and poorly situated stations. It closed in 1959, its latter days providing a home for Class J15 0-6-0s from the Great Eastern (with very tall chimneys), contrasting sharply with a batch of modern Ivatt 2-6-0s delivered new to Kettering shed in 1946 specifically to work the line. My only trip on the railway took place in its latter years when it ran to collect iron ore from a quarry at Twywell. Some kind of minor sensation was provided in 1965 when nothing less than a Jubilee 4-6-0, No. 45660 *Rooke*, was provided for one of these trains, possibly the last run of a Jubilee in everyday BR service on this part of the Midland main line. Kettering also had a secretive line to a quarry at Loddington, reached by dropping down to Cransley (later the site of a well-known George Cohen locomotive scrapyard) and then climbing a fearsome gradient to reach the actual quarry. I was on a brake van rail tour in 1965 that didn't quite make it to the top, the incline defeating it. Yet it was fun trying, the little 2-6-0 blasting with all its might with twelve brake vans until it stalled just short of its destination.

Wellingborough, a few miles south of Kettering, had its own Midland branch to Rushden and Higham Ferrers. This discreetly left Midland Road station and crossed over the Nene Valley Viaduct before swinging off to Rushden. Like other Midland Railway branches, it did not make the Beeching era, closing to passengers in 1959. I remember it as quite a pleasant experience, once home to some strange visiting locomotives that had served their time elsewhere, such as a Lancashire and Yorkshire Railway 2-4-2T that was given a trial, and three ex-Tilbury line 4-4-2 tanks that appeared just after nationalisation. One of these was the now-preserved *Thundersley*, which as No. 41966 had been overhauled with a new boiler in 1949. It was sent to Wellingborough shed and spent three years there in store, before being resurrected for further service and going to Toton for a couple of years. It was then repainted in its old colours and today can be seen at Bressingham Steam Museum in Norfolk.

Back to the LNWR, whose predecessor, the London & Birmingham, built the first railway into Northampton and one of the first British cross-country lines, from Blisworth to Northampton, Wellingborough and Peterborough. It opened in 1845 and according to the local paper there were 'wondrous gazers' there to watch the locomotive and its rudimentary carriages potter along the flat Nene Valley line to Peterborough. The line was expensive to work, with endless level crossings, and Dr Beeching added it to his long list of loss makers. It closed to passengers in May 1964 and the last day trains were a real contrast. That from Peterborough was very busy, but the final service from Wellingborough, augmented to six coaches and run non-stop, had just a handful of passengers – one of them me. With so many people wanting to travel east to west across Britain, either this line or, more likely, that from Rugby to Peterborough, would be a real asset these days.

The LNWR also built a line from Northampton to Market Harborough. This served several ironstone quarries and survived the other Northampton branches by many years. The line ran through pleasant scenery and attractive stations, but this was not enough to save it. However, it also formed an important through route for freights from the East Midlands to the south, so its future seemed assured. Eventually the closure of local ironstone quarries and a decision to re-route through trains ended its life in 1981. There is talk today of it reopening, but there is talk of a lot of railways reopening and most of it, sadly, remains just conjecture.

It is a measure of the decimation of the past that just six of the dozens of stations that once served Northamptonshire still exist, including Corby, which was closed for many years and now thrives with direct services to St Pancras. Kings Sutton also survives, on the Great Western main line, and is a cheeky inclusion in this book as it is on that short stretch of the Paddington to Birmingham route that dips briefly into the county. The Great Central's line through the county, remote and magnificent, has gone completely; Peterborough is still there, of course, but boundary changes have shifted it into Cambridgeshire. What of Northampton itself, often called 'the town that did not want the railway'? Research by Dr Joan Wake and Victor Hatley put that assertion, which I was taught at school, in its proper place. It was civil engineering decisions that caused Robert Stephenson to bypass Northampton as the engines of the day would not have managed the climb out of the town to the north. So he stayed west of the town and even then had to cut through Kilsby Tunnel, which proved a gargantuan task and took the lives of twenty-six navvies.

The county was a source of railway revenue for many years because of its substantial deposits of iron ore. Quarries were dotted around, especially in the Northampton uplands and around Kettering and Wellingborough. We spent many happy days as youngsters shooting the breeze with quarry workers as four- or six-wheeled saddle tanks struggled on poorly laid track with three or four heavily loaded wagons of orange iron ore. They would be assembled into rakes in exchange sidings, where a BR locomotive would take them to the steelworks. Sometimes these would be fairly local, such as the huge plant at Corby, but in the later years Blisworth, for example, was supplying ore to a big steelworks near Wolverhampton.

Most local stations also provided a certain amount of local freight business. Stoke Bruerne, just south of Northampton, is a crazy example. It was open to passengers for only three months way back in the 1890s, but had a siding for freight traffic and remained open for goods traffic for a further sixty years. This was part of the late and much lamented Stratford-upon-Avon & Midland Junction Railway, a freight-carrying byway centred on Towcester that struggled on until the mid-1960s. Northamptonshire also saw huge amounts of freight traffic passing through it, on both main and secondary lines. These comprised long distance freights from South Wales to the East Midlands, endless coal trains running north to south through the county and all kinds of mixed freights of the kind that have completely disappeared, but made our railways so interesting in the 1950s, '60s and '70s.

Today you can still travel along the Midland and West Coast main lines at speeds so fast it's hard to really take in the countryside. Preservation centres at both Rushden and Pitsford and Brampton stations give a flavour of what the Higham Ferrers and Market Harborough lines were like, but their ambitious plans to extend further depend on substantial finance.

It's a tempting to look back to an earlier age and dream of boarding a local train headed by an L1 tank engine at Helmdon Central, alighting at Brackley for afternoon tea in one of the town's delightful cafés. Or maybe standing at Glendon Junction and watching a vast rake of merry-go-round wagons full of coal take the Melton Mowbray line behind a Peak class diesel. Gone, but not forgotten.

Ettrick looks the worse for wear at Blisworth Quarry on 29 April 1979, sporting a cheap coat of blue paint. Despite her appearance she is steam tight and still at work. These are very attractive little Hawthorn Leslie engines.

Class 5 No. 45287 makes a colourful sight at Northampton on 20 September 1965. She still had plenty of service ahead of her, not being withdrawn until August 1968.

A pleasant afternoon with two Stanier engines polluting the atmosphere around Northampton shed. Class 5 No. 45134 and 8F No. 48696 (from Coalville) are seen on 16 September 1965.

In September 1965, Class 8F No. 48637 heads north through Northampton Castle station with a freight for the Market Harborough line.

Class 5 No. 45287 again, this time running light through Northampton in summer 1965.

An unusual combination passes through Northampton, consisting of 8F No. 48349 and Type 4 diesel No. D301 on their way to the engine shed.

A replacement for the withdrawn Jinty steam tanks at Northampton was this jackshaft drive LMS diesel shunter, No. 12009, seen here shunting at the station yard. In the background are long-gone buildings, St Andrew's Church and the Italianate Manfield buildings (far right).

Here are the crew who let us share their cab on Black 5 No. 45190 on the last day of steam at Northampton shed on 25 September 1965. The fireman is Michael Hasdell, with whom I am still in touch, and the driver is Ken Hunt, who died some years ago.

A tough job for a little 'un. Jinty No. 47590 hauls a long transfer freight through Northampton from Far Cotton to Spencer Bridge in July 1965.

A year after most passenger trains in the area were handed over to diesels, Class 5 No. 44863 arrives at Northampton on 2 July 1965 with a train from Rugby. She was allocated to Bletchley (1E).

Some lines cling on long after the first threats of closure were made – like that from Northampton to Market Harborough. But this last train seen in 1981 coming off the branch north of Northampton shows that all efforts to save it have failed. (Bob Mullins)

The last day of the metre-gauge industrial railway at Finedon Quarries on 1 October 1966. Here No. 85, a sturdy 0-6-0ST built by Peckett, is seen in the quarry. No. 85 and her two sisters were preserved.

Peak diesel No. D129 hurries north through a deserted Wellingborough station on 29 September 1966.

On 24 June 1966, Hudswell Clarke 0-6-0ST No. 65 is at the end of an overhaul, completed in the open air at Pitsford Quarries. This work did not include a repaint or knocking the dent out of the smokebox door. She went on to work in a quarry at Crosby, near Scunthorpe.

Deep underneath that grime is green paint, but it is not preventing *Blisworth Mines No. 1* from doing a good job. She is ready to head for the quarry at Blisworth with empties – one of the last two quarries at work in Northamptonshire – on 5 April 1965.

On 31 March 1967, Sulzer Type 2 No. D5006 passes through Piddington with a demolition train on the Northampton to Bedford line. A melancholy duty, but happily the station here survives in the hands of a very caring owner.

Stabled at Northampton station on 12 April 1966 is Type 4 diesel No. D293. The station was in the process of a very uninspiring rebuild. It was quite common to find engines resting here for a few hours.

Lamport ironstone mines, Northamptonshire, on 6 April 1966 with Fowler diesel *Douglas* outside the shed. On this day only steam engines were in use as this 1936 built 0-4-0 was a rather feeble performer.

A noisy departure from Wellingborough station by Class 45 No. D62 *5th Royal Inniskilling Dragoon Guards* on 23 August 1971. The train is heading south past the starter that once contained a signal for the Northampton branch.

At Brackley Town station on 9 April 1965 stood a row of redundant engines, including this very attractive 0-6-0T named *Mesozoic*. She had previously worked at Southam Cement Works with four sisters.

Lamport No. 3 has been driven out of the shed in 1966 for the benefit of the photographer. 'No problem,' said the driver. Quarry lines were like that.

A train of Ford vans heads north through Northampton on its way to Halewood, near Liverpool. Up front is Class AL1 No. E3020 plus an AL6 electric, with an AL3 electric on mineral wagons waiting to follow. The platform has been extended and roughly surfaced at this stage as rebuilding of the station continues. It is 12 May 1966.

Heading south with freight at Draughton on the now closed Northampton to Market Harborough line is ex-works Class 25 No. 7530 on 2 March 1973.

Visitors inspect a train as it leaves the underground mine at Irthlingborough on 1 October 1966. Notice the strange battery-powered locomotive.

An everyday scene at ironstone quarries throughout the Midlands, here at Lamport on 6 April 1966. A Brush Type 4 diesel is about to leave the exchange sidings with the rich red ironstone. Empty wagons have been left for filling.

At Wellingborough Finedon Road were extensive sidings and here Peak Class 45 diesel No. 93 heads north with a train of fitted coal wagons on 10 November 1973. They may be heading for Stewarts and Lloyds at Corby.

The yards at Wellingborough Finedon Road look busy as Sulzer Type 2 No. 5215 runs light towards the station on 10 November 1972.

This was a very pleasant afternoon near Kings Sutton station at the south-western tip of the region. A Presed Steel three-car unit is rumbling past on 6 June 1972, heading for Banbury.

Here is a decent load for a Peak diesel. This long train of coal hoppers is heading for Corby and the engine in charge is No. 130 on 29 September 1972. She is passing Glendon Junction, just north of Kettering, whose church spire can be seen on the skyline.

On 2 March 1973, a pleasant spring morning, Class 47 No. 1631 is seen making its way towards Northampton at Spratton on the line from Market Harborough with three newly overhauled Mk 2 coaches behind.

Northampton Power Station's Bagnall 0-4-0ST is seen here busy shunting on 16 March 1973. Judging by the marks on the tank, at some stage in its life this engine carried a name. The power station closed in 1975.

AM10 electric multiple unit No. 084 arrives at Northampton station with a glimpse of one of Northampton's short-lived single-deck buses crossing Spencer Bridge on 11 May 1973.

Pitsford and Brampton station seen on 21 November 1965, fifteen years after closure. It is now the headquarters of the Northampton & Lamport heritage railway. (Bryan Jeyes)

Class AL3 electric locomotive No. E3029 at Northampton Castle station, waiting to depart with an excursion to Blackpool on 29 May 1966. (Bryan Jeyes)

Standing at the closed Byfield Mines in Northamptonshire on 4 April 1966 is Bagnall 0-6-0ST *Cherwell*. She was later transported to a playground in Daventry, a rather ignominious fate for such a nice engine. Now she is in the care of the enthusiasts at Rushden station, but restoration is probably a long way off.

On 14 January 1973 we are at the point where the West Coast main line separates at Roade, with the slow lines going towards Northampton and the fast line direct to Rugby. A passenger train headed by Class AL6 No. E3171 is taking the Northampton route.

A Peak class diesel is seen south of Kettering in 1983 at an interim stage of modernisation – old telegraph poles still there, but new signalling in place. (Bob Mullins)

Nottinghamshire

Coal mining and manufacturing defined this county, which sprouted a complex network of railways north of the city of Nottingham. All three main players in the county wanted to get their share of such prolific traffic and although the railway map was dominated by Midland red, the Great Central ran its main spine from Nottingham to Sheffield and the Great Northern had a north to south line between Nottingham and Langwith Junction, also serving coal mines. This was Britain's largest coal field and in the 1960s, as you travelled on main or secondary routes by passenger train, there were endless sidings and small yards with all kinds of LMS, LNER, WD and BR Standard freight engines keeping the coal moving. Much of it headed south along the Midland, Great Northern and Great Central main lines. At Wellingborough in Northamptonshire, the lineside watcher in the early 1960s would see a steady procession of long unfitted mineral wagons loaded with coal trudging south behind 9Fs, Stanier 8Fs and quite a few 4F 0-6-0s. (The free-flowing Great Central ran the same trains at more than twice the speed.) This was Nottinghamshire's countryside on the move, and it did not leave a very pretty landscape behind. Much has been done since then to improve the scenic appearance and the old mining towns have found new reasons for existence. Returning north was an equally busy flow of empties.

During the contraction of our railways during the 1960s and 1970s, the local and main line passenger and freight services in north Nottinghamshire were particularly badly affected. The Great Central main line disappeared completely along with most other GC routes, although the part of the Sheffield to Retford line that skirted north Nottinghamshire has always remained open for passengers. The Great Northern's freight lines were also swept away, except for that section of the East Coast main line that penetrated the county. The Midland's vast array of lines was reduced to what was basically a main line from Toton to Chesterfield, the Derby to Nottingham line, and a selection of other railways that remained open to serve coal mines. This left Mansfield, once blessed with three stations, as the largest town in the country with no railway station, although in 1995 the Nottingham to Worksop route reopened to passengers as the Robin Hood line and the handsome Mansfield Town station came back to life with it. Mansfield was not unique; several other towns like Hucknall also benefitted from three stations, with all three succumbing. In the end there were simply too many railways and too many stations in that area between Mansfield and Chesterfield. Even without Dr Beeching, such intensity of lines and services could not survive.

Back in the 1960s major depots like Langwith Junction and Annesley and many smaller centres acted as handling points for freight. These were rather like the hubs used by airlines. A visit to a freight shed like Annesley at the weekend would reveal around sixty engines; Langwith Junction might have fifty and there was a flurry of smaller sheds throughout the county, many serving local coal mines. When our little group visited Kirkby-in-Ashfield on a Wednesday morning in 1964 we saw a vast number of Stanier 8Fs and Standard 9Fs. There were many other depots just like it, mainly hosting freight engines, with a smattering of tanks for local services. Kirkby became another town to lose all three stations and when the Robin Hood line was reopened, a completely new station had to be built.

The impact of coal mining upon the economy and the landscape of Nottinghamshire was huge. Such mining also meant instability and subsidence caused frequent speed restrictions. New mines were still being opened well after the Second World War. For example, Calverton, although started before the war, was not opened until 1952 and was served by a new spur just south of Hucknall. When it closed in 1999 it was one of the last collieries in Nottinghamshire, although Thoresby, in north Nottinghamshire, survived until 2015. It was served by a spur from the Great Central line east of Shirebrook.

From Bagthorpe to Sutton-in-Ashfield, the three railways shared a north–south corridor with passenger trains, locals and freights clustered together. Many of the collieries were near villages, so some of these had more than one station. When closures before (often many years before) and after Beeching ripped through this area, the heart of industrial Nottinghamshire's railways was torn away and by the 1980s only the Midland line, Great Central freight lines around Edwinstowe and part of the Great Northern remained. The prime casualty, of course, was the Great Central, but south and east of Chesterfield a huge array of lines, mainly Great Central, were closed.

The city of Nottingham itself became a very busy railway centre and was attractive for enthusiasts because of its two main lines, the Midland and Great Central, and many local railways. The Midland firstly looked south to its all-important link to London. Then it spread its tentacles outwards to Lincoln, through the Erewash Valley and north Mansfield. Eventually it reached Derby and Melton Mowbray.

The Midland was not destined to have it all its own way. One can only speculate about its reaction when the Great Northern trains entered from Grantham and the east into the heart of the city and, audaciously, managed to offer a service from the city to London quicker than the Midland. As Howard Anderson recalls, 'This was too much for the Midland,' who seem to have hijacked the train and held it hostage for seven months – and we think today's corporate companies sometime play dirty.

Eventually the Great Northern built its own route right into Nottingham and also a line that curved neatly around the north of Nottingham, linking with the Great Central at Bagthorpe Junction, and then running west through Ilkeston and into Derbyshire. From there they headed north to seize a share of the coalfield traffic. Always a line that suffered from subsidence, parts were abandoned pre-Beeching, but in its day it was a vital freight artery and also carried important local passenger traffic.

The Manchester, Sheffield & Lincolnshire Railway, with delusions of grandeur, was working its way south and west together with its partner, the Great Northern. Together they built Nottingham Victoria, a kind of transport cathedral, accessed through a vast infrastructure. The MSL simply built across the top of Nottingham to gain entry to its new station, which was in a deep cutting right in the centre of the city. Passengers waiting for trains at the Midland Railway station had an excellent view of Great Central expresses passing symbolically above them on a mighty girder bridge, before plunging into the vast and opulent Victoria station. If anything said 'We mean business' it was the newly named Great Central's sweeping silver metals through Nottingham. Passengers could also head east by the Great Northern to Grantham and, rather tortuously, to Melton Mowbray and Northampton using the splendid joint line already mentioned. But most of them would journey south to Leicester, Rugby and Marylebone. Recalling the early closure of the Great Central route still brings a lump to the throat. There was a very clear and deliberate run down of services. Was it the old Midland trying to get its own back, or was the quite obvious duplication of routes through the East Midlands enough of an item on the balance sheet to prompt a speedy closure of the old Great Central? Initially we were told that Victoria station would stay. Then it would be removed, but two through tracks would remain. Then ... nothing. One thing is sure, however: when the fast freights were routed away from the Great Central they simply evaporated. Although we cannot expect people in the 1960s to be have been visionaries, how useful would the route be today? I was hired by a company to do some publicity for their project in the early 2000s to reopen part of the Great Central as a freight route, but this was turned down by the government. There always seem to be new schemes to rebuild the Great Central. Maybe we all secretly know this will not happen.

Toton depot specialised in celebrity locomotives like No. 44008 *Penyghent*, seen here in 1979 at Stoke heading for home.

A Sulzer Type 2 passes through Nottingham's wonderful Victoria station in its dying days on 8 October 1966. (Bryan Jeyes)

A Class 8F from Annesley shed, No. 48170 passes light through a deserted Nottingham Victoria station on 8 October 1966. (Bryan Jeyes)

Looking south from the Midland Railway's Basford Vernon station in the northern suburbs of Nottingham on 8 October 1966. This section now forms part of the revived Robin Hood line from Nottingham to Mansfield. (Bryan Jeyes)

Kegworth station on the Midland main line north of Loughborough a few days before closure. A diesel unit calls on 24 February 1968. (Bryan Jeyes)

Weekday Cross Junction where the Grantham route left the main Great Central main line. From here, to the left, a tunnel ran to Nottingham Victoria station. (Bryan Jeyes)

The English Electric Type 1s could be seen all over the Nottingham area in the 1970s. Here we have a very grubby pair, Nos 8006 and 8171, running through Nottingham Midland station with a freight on 1 September 1972. The newer locomotive is in green and the older one in blue.

Thompson B1 4-6-0 No. 61406 running east through Edwinstowe, Nottinghamshire, with the LCGB Notts and Lincs special train to Immingham shed on 24 April 1965. (John Cosford)

Class O4/7 2-8-0 No. 63843 from Langwith Junction is running west through Edwinstowe, Nottinghamshire, with a train of mineral wagons on 24 April 1965. Edwinstowe station closed on 2 January 1956, after which the footbridge and platform canopies were removed. (John Cosford)

Kirkby Bentinck station, on the Nottingham to Sheffield main line, looking west in April 1965. The station was built by the Manchester, Sheffield & Lincolnshire Railway and opened in 1893. Its name reflected the proximity of the nearby Bentinck colliery. The station closed to all traffic in March 1963. (John Cosford)

On the RCTS's Eight Counties rail tour from Northampton is Colwick B1 No. 61302. She is seen here at Shirebrook North on 26 March 1966 and it was her last run. She was withdrawn the next day.

Class O4/7 2-8-0 No. 63691 is heading east light engine at Clipstone Junction with a sister O4/8 on 24 April 1965. She was allocated to Langwith Junction shed (41J) and was withdrawn one month later. (John Cosford)

Class 44 No. D4 *Great Gable* is seen heading south a month or so prior to its withdrawal at Trent in November 1980. (Bob Mullins)

On 2 November 1979 a Class 56 passes Trent with coal for Ratcliffe-on-Soar Power Station. (Bob Mullins)

More coal and another Class 56 passing Trent, this time heading for Castle Donington Power Station. (Bob Mullins)

Our last Class 56 picture is on the high-level goods line near Trent with the engine heading south in 1979. (Bob Mullins)

On 20 September 1967 the forecourt canopy of Victoria station has gone as the demolition men destroy this fine building. (Bryan Jeyes)

Rutland

Small but perfectly formed, Rutland still has part of its admittedly small railway network intact. Bounded on the west by the joint line through Leicestershire, on the north by the Midland link to the Midland and Great Northern Joint (both of which have gone), the main routes through the county are still there. These are the Leicester to Peterborough North line, with its station at Oakham (the only station in the county) and the main Kettering to Melton Mowbray route, now principally a freight line. The Great Northern main line cuts through the western corner, but there are no stations. The lost routes centred on Seaton are covered separately.

Entering Seaton station with a westbound train on 4 June 1966 is Type 2 diesel No. D5036. The track is weedy, but otherwise there are few clues that is the last day of train services. In the background the lines go straight ahead to Stamford (the original route) and right to Peterborough north.

The rarely photographed Rutland Railway Museum in 1985, based at Cottesmore on a Midland Railway mineral branch. It is now known as Rocks by Rail. (Bob Mullins).

Five years after closure, Uppingham station is in a sad state of disrepair on 4 June 1966. Can you imagine a Tilbury tank waiting to leave for Seaton?

Sulzer Type 2 No. D5036 leaves Seaton for Market Harborough on 4 June 1966, the last day of services. The little wreath is a nice touch. (Bryan Jeyes)

Peak diesel No. D2 Helvellyn hauls a northbound freight across the Welland Viaduct on 4 June 1966. (Bryan Jeyes).

On 7 July 1972 at Essendine No. 1515, a Brush Class 47, races past with a train of blue and grey Metro-Cammell Pullmans forming the Tees Tyne Pullman for Kings Cross.

The north end of the Welland Viaduct is in Rutland and here No. 50048 *Dauntless* and No. 50010 *Monarch* heading the Derby Double rail tour on 18 March 1978. The tour ran from Paddington to Derby and Matlock and return. (Bob Mullins)

Seaton station's sign with a Class 47 in the distance crossing the Welland Viaduct in 1966.

Ketton and Collyweston station between Seaton and Stamford with its narrow platforms on 4 June 1966. Nothing suggests this is the final day of train services.

This is the Seaton branch train waiting to leave Seaton after its takeover by diesel units. The route to Seaton (and, once, Uppingham) goes straight on. Notice the large water tank, the crossover halfway along the platforms and the weedy track. Very pleasant scenery with cows in the fields on a typical English summer day. What could be nicer?

A picture taken behind Class 47 No. 47459 as it powers across the Welland Viaduct on 15 September 1985 with a Corbyrail special from Kettering to Llandudno. (Bob Mullins)

Motive Power, Steam and Diesel

We have already seen how the Midland Railway dominated the landscape in the East Midlands. This continued right through to British Railways days, when, despite the widespread use of LMS and BR Standard steam locomotives, Fowler and Deeley engines were still a very common sight almost to the end of steam. Some Johnson 0-6-0 tank engines, a type built between 1878 and 1892, clung to life at Staveley Ironworks in north Derbyshire until 1965, the result of a bizarre arrangement that stemmed from the Midland Railway's decision in 1866 to sign an agreement to provide shunting engines at the works for 100 years. As these ancient 0-6-0s were the most suitable engines, they survived long into the diesel age and I was very sad to see one lined up at Cransley scrapyard, near Kettering, awaiting its fate with types built sixty years later. Happily, another of them, No. 41708, was rescued for preservation.

During the period under review, from 1965 until 1985, steam made a fairly quick exit. Yet one of the final outposts of steam was in north Derbyshire, where Stanier 2-8-0s were at work into 1968 operating heavy limestone hoppers to the works at Tunstead. When Buxton shed closed in March 1968 it marked the virtual end of steam in the East Midlands, although rail tours and odd incursions still took place after that. Counties south of Derbyshire had gradually lost steam from 1965 onwards. As steam retrenched, we would have to travel farther and farther afield from our home base at Northampton. Yet even in 1965 there was a steady procession of steam-hauled freight trains passing through Derby, headed by Standard and LMS types. Veteran Midland Railway-built Fowler 0-6-0s were still at work, no fewer than sixteen of them finding employment on local freight trains. Several of the last survivors were based at Westhouses near Alfreton, Derbyshire, a noted freight depot.

Besides the Peaks, other types of diesel were widespread, mainly the BR Sulzer Type 2 of Classes 24 and 25. These became synonymous with the East Midlands and could be seen almost anywhere in the late 1960s. Despite their modest size, they were sometimes entrusted with important expresses. These included Bradford to St Pancras trains, which were rostered for a Class 25 quite often in 1966. The other type in general use, especially in Nottinghamshire and Derbyshire, was the English Electric Class 20, a pioneer of the BR Modernisation Plan. Toton depot hosted a big fleet – more than 100 at its maximum in the 1970s – and the two counties could be relied on by spotters to produce endless lines of freight trains all headed by a pair of Class 20s, coupled nose to nose. For several years they were also used on excursions to Skegness in the summer. By the mid-1980s, the era of the early diesels was coming to a close. The Deltic had already disappeared from the East Coast main line; Peak diesels had started to be replaced by high-speed trains in the early 1980s, and by 1985 were becoming increasingly rare. I was living in Nuneaton at the time and there was an evening working from Leicester that brought one of the survivors to our town. When it was known that this service was to be taken over by other motive power, a large group of enthusiasts gathered at Nuneaton station to pay our last respects. Alas, ironically the Peak gave trouble and was replaced by a Brush Class 31.

Like everywhere else on our railways at the time, the Brush Type 4 (Class 47) became ubiquitous. They saw off the end of steam and then dealt a mortal blow to lesser, if sometimes more fascinating, modern power. As older types were withdrawn, the sheer utility of the Class 47 showed the virtues of a robust, well-proven design that did most things well and met the needs of the operating department and those sitting in the cab. While technologically unadventurous, the go-almost-anywhere, haul-almost-anything approach of the Class 47 meant that in the East Midlands they became a very familiar site. In 1966 I saw a brand-new Class 47 locomotive hauling an express for Nottingham through Market Harborough. Some twelve years later the same engine was passing Beeston with a row of oil tanks, and in 1985 it was back in the East Midlands, this time hauling an excursion on the Midland main line through Loughborough. In the end it gave forty years' service. Unsurprisingly, the Class 47 makes a regular appearance in these pages. Later came the Class 56 freight engines, which after a slightly inauspicious start settled down to give such long service that a number are working today.

This was also the age of the multiple unit. By the mid-1960s they could be seen everywhere and on one occasion in 1973 at Derby station I saw ten of them on different trains, some coupled together, others as two-car units, all breathing fumes as they awaited business. It was also the age of the diesel shunter, but as freight yards closed and the nature of freight traffic changed from wagon loads to containers and block formations, the friendly old 08s were gradually withdrawn.

Many of the types that served the East Midlands during the 'classic years' are illustrated in this volume and I apologise if your favourite is not among them.

The Thames-Clyde Express

Unlike the rival West and East Coast routes, where named trains flew past with great regularity in the 1950s, Midland main line customers enjoyed very few named expresses. The main ones were the Palatine, the Robin Hood, the Waverley and the Thames-Clyde Express. Later came the Master Cutler, inherited from the Great Central line when its expresses were withdrawn in 1958; it then ran as a Pullman train to Kings Cross, but was finally relaunched as a new train in 1969 on the Midland main line.

Although the Palatine had a history going back to 1938, the Robin Hood and Waverley were children of the 1950s explosion of named trains. But the Thames-Clyde Express was the granddaddy of this group, running for the first time in 1927 between Glasgow and St Pancras. It left St Pancras shortly after 10.00 and ran up the Midland main line to Luton, Kettering and Leicester where it stopped. It then continued to Nottingham Midland, reversed and headed north to Chesterfield, Sheffield Midland, Leeds, Carlisle and after three stops in Scotland reached Glasgow St Enoch (later Central) after well over eight hours of travel. Now, obviously, if you were sitting in either London or Glasgow, you would hardly choose the leisurely Thames-Clyde Express over the speedy West Coast services, so most passengers were using it for only part of its journey. This included me in 1973. I decided it would be interesting to go to Carlisle using the Thames-Clyde Express, so I presented myself at Kettering station late one morning and a grubby Peak diesel, No. 119, duly arrived under the station's elegant awnings towing nine Mk 1 coaches. I scrambled aboard along with a dozen or so other passengers to enjoy an experience all too familiar to those who patronise heritage railways, where Mk 1s, with their bouncy seat springs and excellent visibility, give a characterful ride. No. 119 may have looked a bit down at heel, but there was nothing wrong with her mechanical condition, and we made a bright start up to Glendon Junction, taking the left route to Market Harborough and Leicester. In those days the Midland main line had not changed much since steam days, being lined with those vast telegraph poles and a forest of semaphore signalling.

Having extracted her train from the gloom of Leicester London Road, No. 119 put on a creditable show and arrived at Nottingham a couple of minutes down. Here No. 119 was retired for a lunchtime snooze and sister engine No. D87 arrived to take charge. (This was the era when BR was getting rid of 'D' in front of diesel numbers.) We left a few minutes late, passing beneath the Great Central overbridge and then heading north to Chesterfield in days when there were several speed restrictions due to mining subsidence. But D87 did a good job, catching up on its lost time to Leeds and then giving us a very spirited run over the Settle–Carlisle line to arrive in Glasgow on time. Yet another Peak was produced for the final run to Glasgow: No. 42, in very clean condition. But I left the train at Carlisle. By now it was late afternoon and the economics of the service were baffling to me. We had used three different locomotives, wandered happily around the East Midlands and finally made it to the Scottish border. It was certainly a useful service from the East Midlands to Scotland, but it wasn't a great surprise when it was announced that as from 3 May 1975, the Thames-Clyde Express would cease to run. By the time I made my journey, the 'express' had honestly lost the right to that designation. It was little more than a long-distance, cross-country stopping train. But it marked the beginning of the end of British Rail trains that would connect the East Midlands directly with the north and Scotland. Happily, Cross Country Trains now offer just such a service but not using the Midland main line. I am just sorry I was a bit too young to use the Waverley (to Edinburgh) and the Palatine (to Manchester) before they ceased to run in the 1960s.

The Thames-Clyde Express arrives at Kettering on 10 May 1973, the occasion of the journey related above.

The Midland Pullman

The Midland Pullman (and its Western Region sisters) is probably more important for what it led to than for the service it provided. In 1960 the new trains took to the rails, providing upmarket travel for the business community from Manchester to St Pancras utilising a six-coach, air-conditioned diesel set with a fixed rake of vehicles. The similar Western Region units comprised eight vehicles. With staff arrayed in white coats and the trains painted a handsome Nanking Blue with the Pullman crest on the front, everything looked set for a triumphant launch. There were teething troubles. The ride of the Metro-Cammel units left a lot to be desired and the start time from Manchester meant business travellers did not arrive in the capital until midday. But some of these issues were corrected and for six years the train gave good service, until replaced by an electric locomotive-hauled West Coast route Pullman service that was much faster. Meals were sumptuous and expensive for their time and the standard of accommodation was quite exceptional when compared with ordinary stock or the classic Pullman service used on other lines. A full meal service was provided to every passenger. One problem was knowing what to do with the train between reaching St Pancras and setting off back to Manchester in the evening. It was therefore decided to offer a lunchtime service to Nottingham, which we used to see regularly heading there and back, often virtually empty. A spare set had to be kept on standby, which was very wasteful on resources. However, the Midland Pullman pointed the way forward for British express travel. The HST was also a fixed-formation, high-speed diesel set and owed much to the concept of the Midland Pullman, but with a great deal more power.

Britain's Last Push-pull Train

Seaton station sits quietly in the Rutland countryside, with distant views of the vast Harringworth Viaduct. In its day it was an important junction. It was here that the Rugby to Peterborough line, a busy through line for summer expresses from the West Midlands to the holiday resorts of East Anglia, offered passengers a chance to change for Stamford and Uppingham, two branches worked mainly by push-pull services. The Uppingham service, not opened until 1894, proved to be quite short-lived, closing in 1960 shortly before the Beeching revolution. It had latterly seen five trains a day, often requiring just one coach and worked by a Standard or Ivatt 2-6-2 tank, but – as mentioned earlier – a fascinating interloper was an ex-Tilbury line 4-4-2T that was also used on these trains. A bit of a comedown for these excellent engines, which did so much good work hauling heavy trains from London to Southend and then found themselves pottering around the rural and undulating East Midlands with one basically empty coach. Not being push-pull fitted, they ran round at the ramshackle Uppingham terminus, with its oversized canopy, tall chimneys and neglected flower beds – it hadn't seen a lick of paint for quite a few years. The old LNWR-style 'Hawkseye' station name board sat not on the platform, but across the two tracks on the grass opposite. Hardly convenient for those looking out of the window at the station side to see where they were. But I guess they knew the train only went to Uppingham.

More important was the line to Stamford, which was an early venture, going back to 1850. In fact, this was the original route of the Rugby line. If you stood on Seaton station the Peterborough lines swung to the right, eventually joining the Northampton to Peterborough route (which now forms part of the Nene Valley heritage railway) while the Stamford route went straight ahead.

Let's recall a ride back in early 1965. Stamford trains started from the bay platform at Seaton, where our Standard tank and two push-pull coaches slumbered quietly in the midday sunshine. Connections with trains heading between Rugby and Peterborough were not great – as usual I had a long wait to catch the Stamford service. Still, it was worth it. There was no sign of the crew, but a few minutes before departure they appeared, bustling around in the cab and getting ready to leave. Dare I ask for a ride in the cab? Alas, no. But I chatted with them and found myself to be the only passenger on a winter day in early 1965. Our locomotive, No. 84008, suddenly showed signs of life, a trickle of steam appearing around the safety valve. The guard blew his whistle and we headed out of the bay and on to the main line. Leaving the Peterborough route, we accelerated away and settled into the rhythmic hiss and clank of progress. The Stamford route passed beneath the main Kettering to Melton Mowbray route and then the remnants of the Uppingham branch. Then we entered Morcott tunnel, just under 500 yards long, through a massive and impressive horseshoe-shaped portal, exiting into a deep cutting before reaching Morcott's wooden single platform. Originally, this section was double track, but it had been singled for many years. Inside the tunnel, the track was slewed to one side.

At Morcott station the maroon station name boards turned to dark blue, showing we had entered the Eastern Region. (But the station woodwork was still finished in maroon – very odd!) The small station building (with toilets) faced a wooden platform and there were brackets on the front of the building, suggesting that once there had been a canopy.

We picked up a few passengers (Morcott was a staffed station, amazingly) and soon moved off, joining the main Leicester to Peterborough railway and entering Luffenham station. This was a very elegant building, but on this day produced no passengers. Next came a quick run to our next station, Ketton and Collyweston, while a Brush Type 4 passed in the opposite direction with a long, mixed freight. Ketton was a very odd station as the platforms were amazingly narrow. Yet the buildings were very handsome. The stationmaster produced a few more passengers for us and soon we were back on our way, this time on the last leg of our journey. Our tank engine was soon slowing for the entry into Stamford's wonderful old grey stone station. Quite apart from the architecture with its distinctive pointed turret, it had (and still has for the most part) lots to interest railway types. At the east end of the platforms was a starting and

No. 84008 waits patiently for departure at Seaton.

distant signal mounted on a structure that spanned both tracks. Then came a couple of bridges and a tunnel, from which in steam days trains emerged shrouded in smoke. On the opposite platform for many years there was an old LNER brake composite coach, painted black and, if my memory serves allocated to a welding team. On the opposite platform was a bay, to which, after setting down all its passengers, No. 84008 retired. This was guarded by what must have been one of the shortest signals in Britain, nestling against a steep embankment. Having earned a rest, after a brief burst (about 25 minutes) of energy, both No. 84008 and its crew returned to their siesta. The crew found lunch and No. 84008 dozed. I glanced in the cab while waiting for the return journey. Looking back, it was amazing how steam engines were so often left unoccupied at platforms for long periods. You couldn't lock the cab, so everyone was trusted not to do anything stupid. Even if you clambered on board for a quick look round, chances were nobody would be too bothered.

This was my last journey on a steam train from Seaton to Stamford. In October 1965 Nos 84005, 84006, 84008 and 41219 and her sisters were parked up at Leicester shed ready for scrap and their duties were taken over by a two-car diesel multiple unit, complete with a steam-age oil lamp on the back. Actually, this wasn't all bad, as in those days you could sit up front and enjoy a driver's view. But it soon became clear that providing a train service from Seaton to Stamford for a bod with a camera (me) and four or five shoppers was *not* the future of East Midlands travel. What was much more of a surprise was that the comparatively busy through route from Rugby to Peterborough was to get the axe as well – Dr Beeching took no prisoners. On Saturday 4 June 1966 we took our last, sombre journeys on both the Rugby to Peterborough and Seaton to Stamford branches. For this last day I loaded my camera with colour film and you can see the results in this book. And so a very characteristic and attractive set of East Midlands railway lines died, leaving only happy memories.

Ironstone Quarrying

Much of the East Midlands bears the scars of more than a hundred years of ironstone quarrying. There were – according to historian Eric Tonks – three main areas. One covered most of Lincolnshire. A second included Leicestershire and Rutland, while the third was based on Northamptonshire and Oxfordshire. Giant draglines could be seen poking above the landscape, stripping away the iron ore in layers. It would then be moved by an internal railway to exchange sidings where British Railways provided a locomotive to take it away for smelting. Thanks to this industry, BR derived much income and long trains of mineral wagons could be seen throughout the region. Sometimes the journey to the steelworks might be fairly short (to Corby or Scunthorpe, perhaps), while other trips were much longer (to furnaces in Yorkshire or South Wales). The industry that started so abruptly – in the mid-1850s and probably in Northamptonshire – disappeared equally quickly. Although in the 1950s it enjoyed a burst of prosperity, reduced demand for iron in the 1960s saw the industry collapse, and after 1970 just a couple of East Midlands quarries were still at work.

The railways built by the quarry owners were all fascinating and all different. Tracks were lifted and moved regularly according to where the dragline was. They were also friendly places where you were generally welcomed if you showed an interest and took modest safety precautions. Happily, some of the engines seen at work in these pictures are now enjoying a new life in preservation.

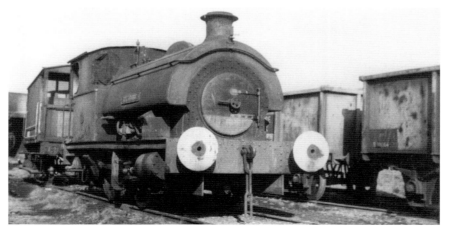

Ettrick at Blisworth– she was sold for preservation to someone who turned out to be a scrap merchant.

Conclusion

The pictures in this book take you on a journey – in many ways the personal journey of the photographers involved, rather than an exhaustive attempt to cover every part of the region. I was based in Northampton and loved nothing more than wandering around old, derelict stations or striding across a muddy field to photograph a little tank engine at an ironstone quarry. I travelled widely in the early 1970s, photographing diesels and electrics. Bryan Jeyes proved an indefatigable photographer of the last days of the Great Central, plus turning his attention to many oddly endearing stations in Leicestershire and Nottinghamshire that were about to close. His colour shots are a prized and fascinating record of a world that disappeared so very fast, and he has allowed me to plunder many previously unpublished pictures from his archive. Bob Mullins always loved Deltics, but he also travelled around creatively photographing everything from quarry railways to some of the better (and lesser) known East Midlands railway haunts. I am also grateful to David Hird, who helped with some excellent pictures in Lincolnshire, and to John Cosford, who sought out images of the last of steam in north Nottinghamshire, a real gap in my collection. Lastly, my wife Jane proved invaluable in checking and editing all the text and captions. Any errors are nevertheless mine. We hope you enjoy travelling on this pictorial journey with us.

Bibliography

Evans, J., *Great Central Railway: Decline and Fall* (Stroud: Amberley Publishing, 2020)

Hatley, V., 'Northampton Revindicated' in *Northamptonshire Past and Present*, Vol. 2, No. 6 (Northampton: Northamptonshire Record Society, 1959)

Hamilton Ellis, C., *The Trains We Loved* (London: George Allen & Unwin, 1947)

Howard Anderson, P., *Forgotten Railways, The East Midlands* (Newton Abbot: David & Charles, 1973)

Lambert, A., *East Midlands Branch Line Album* (Shepperton: Ian Allan Publishing, 1978)

Leleux, R., *A Regional History of the Railways of Great Britain, Volume 9: The East Midlands* (Newton Abbot: David & Charles, 1976)

Longworth, H., *BR Steam Locomotives 1948–1968* (Hersham: Ian Allan Publishing, 2014)

Marsden, C., *British Rail Motive Power 1984* (London: Ian Allan Publishing, 1984)

Tonks, E., *The Ironstone Quarries of the Midlands Part 1* (Cheltenham: Runpast Publishing, 1988)

Wake, J., *Northampton Vindicated or Why the Main Line Missed the Town* (Northampton: Joan Wake, 1935)